DON'T LET ANYBODY STEAL YOUR DREAM

DEXTER R. YAGER SR.

interNET

PUBLISHED BY INTERNET SERVICES CORPORATION
CHARLOTTE, NC

CONTENTS

1

♦♦♦

DON'T LET ANYBODY
STEAL YOUR DREAM

Our lives are shaped by dreams. What and where we are today is a result of dreams come true. Every building you see has sprung from someone's imagination. Every shopping center and the stores in them, every vehicle has first been someone's vision. Stop and think, everything we touch is a result of dreams come true. So dreaming can be a very healthy practice. Woodrow Wilson said, "We grow great by dreams. All big men are dreamers. They see things in the soft haze of a spring day, or in the red fire on a long winter's evening. Some of us let these great dreams die, but others nourish and protect them; nourish them through bad days till they bring them to the sunshine and light which comes always to those who sincerely hope that their dreams will come true."

A positive imagination is very important. It is a road map to success. No one would leave on a long trip to some unfamiliar location without first consulting a map. Likewise, those who have no dreams or goals for which to strive, wander aimlessly, never accomplishing anything of much value.

Dreams are God-given and need to be nourished. Sadly enough, many allow life to rob them of their dreams. The thief comes in the form of many people and circumstances. Your parents, friends, associates, and colleagues may unknowingly and innocently steal your dreams. "What makes you think you can do that?" they will say. "It won't work. That's impossible. Give up on that idea." But if it's your vision, your prayer, your dream why give up so easily? Give it a chance and never let someone else make the decision for you and destroy it!

Of course, I am not suggesting that every dream is practical and that every idea is a sound one. Neither am I suggesting that the opinions of others are not to be considered. Remember, however, that this is your vision. It is the product of your own subconscious, it is almost an instinct. Trust it awhile! If your dream is wrong you will find out soon enough, but if it is right and you don't try, you may lose a lifetime of rewards.

I suggest a counter-attack! When someone puts you down, don't stay down, reverse it. The road to success is not well paved. You have to work for success by planning your own route. There will be those who constantly put you down and other obstacles that arise along the way. Reverse the situations and rise above the difficulties, keeping in mind that someone has to cut the trees down first. For every dream that is carried through, thousands are stolen. To be a winner we need to rise above criticism. We need to be like postage stamps that "stick to it" until we arrive at our goals.

As a boy I always wanted to have a business of my own. That was an early goal. My mom would encourage me, "Yagers just don't work for someone else that good. They've gotta be their own boss." You see, she conditioned me in an effective manner. She programmed my computer in a very positive way. Her words rang in my ears. I then made up my mind that I was going to accomplish my goal.

I always had a business mind. In 1949, while in the sixth grade, I proved to myself and to others my ability to conduct a business. I got the idea of buying soda pop for five cents a bottle, and then turning around and selling it for a dime to construction workers. There were no vending machines nearby and the workers couldn't take off work to visit the store. I was offering them a service as well as a product. I used the ice from my mother's refrigerator. Immediately, my business was a success. I started selling cases of pop. I soon learned that I could go to a wholesale place and in turn, make a much larger profit from my sales.

At first my little business struck people as "cute." Soon I was earning more than most adults. Word passed around town and some businessmen thought that it was time to take over my little operation. They came in with their own ice and drinks. Wherever I set up, they set up too and soon they were all over the city, much bigger than me.

I learned a cruel lesson. Nobody else will fight for your dream. My customers, who thought me an aggressive boy and admired my hard work were very fickle. I thought they were my friends and would stick by me. The truth was they only respected the price and availability of the drinks.

Even my supportive mother thought I had had a good thing for awhile, I should be thankful, but now it was over. It was unnatural for a youngster to make that kind of money. Imagine, the whole world was standing by watching adults gang up on a little kid's dream. If I wanted to keep my business I had to fight.

That's what I did. I hired help. We worked harder. We poured more drinks for the price. We had a better selection. And on hot days we made sure we never ran out of ice. We won the war, our competition ran away. For them it was just another business venture, but to me it was a dream come true

9

and I had to fight to keep it.

Joseph, the beloved son of Jacob, also was a big dreamer. As a boy many of his days were spent tending his father's flocks and dreaming. Daily he meditated upon the God of Israel and daily he dreamed big dreams. In his excitement he would share with his brothers what he had dreamed.

They soon began to despise his "holier-than-thou" proclamations. Joseph, in all honesty, did not intend to reflect that kind of attitude. He simply shared with his brothers hoping to gain their enthusiasm. He very innocently wanted them to share in his joys and aspirations. Joseph allowed his heart and mind to become reservoirs of God's infilling. In all probability, Joseph was a highly motivated young man. His goals were well established, he knew what he wanted in life and the general direction he was headed. No one was going to steal his dreams. Yet his brothers resented and despised him. Their mediocre, slothful ambitions looked poor in light of his. They had no self-fixed goals. Father Jacob had much land and their futures were secure, so farming well suited them. When they could no longer stand to hear their father and neighbors sing his praises, Joseph's brothers formed a conspiracy to kill him, and rid themselves of this obnoxious threat. At the last minute they changed their minds and instead, sold him into slavery thinking that to be the end of their pesty brother. After this terrible ordeal, Joseph was still determined to live out his dreams. Pursuing events prove his unbending spirit.

Adverse circumstances cause many to concede their dreams. They lose perspective of their overall goals, settle for second best—exactly what Joseph's eleven brothers did. Imprisonment, false accusations, years of time, lonely days did not deter Joseph. Rather, he was strengthened to more forcefully pursue his goals. And he did. All of his adverse circumstances turned around for good. In other words, Joseph reversed the situation and rose above the difficulties.

Consider this, it wasn't what Joseph went through, or even

what he accomplished, but it was who he knew that helped him reach his goals. First, Joseph knew the God of Israel. He wished only to live a life pleasing to His sight. You did not ask to be here, God put you here. You must believe that He has a purpose. Your goals, like Joseph's are God-given and God-driven.

Secondly, Joseph knew himself. He knew his potential, his limitations, he recognized the motivational pull in his life, and clung to available resources. His computer had been programmed properly. Father Jacob saw to that. In the midst of family turmoil and strife he displayed self-assurance and a positive image. Those credentials paved his way toward success.

Finally, while in prison he met direct contacts that eventually referred him to the Pharaoh. In accordance, as a boy Joseph dreamed of political prominence. He pictured himself a ruler. "Behold, the sun and the moon and the stars made obessiance to me," he explained to his brothers one day.

Another personal attribute that worked toward Joseph's success was his ability and willingness to start at the bottom. At seventeen he was but a lowly shepherd. Within 23 years he reigned second to Pharaoh in the Egyptian domain. His God-give dream became reality—Joseph was a political figurehead.

Up to the time that Birdie and I were married I worked in the sales department at Sears and Roebuck. For many years after, I was a car salesman. Often my customers spoke condescendingly, they portrayed a superior attitude. I was not intimidated by them. I did not react, either with defensive anger or with passive self-pity. None of them, not one, could compare to my dream. I would willingly and cheerfully take their money to reach my goals. Today approximately 50,000 independent distributors comprise Yager Enterprises. We sell practically everything under the sun, including a multiple line of household products. We've only come this far because we were determined to rise above the difficulties we faced,

11

reverse the situations, and do something great in our lives.

Joseph carried that same determination. While he was experiencing prominence and success in Egypt, back in Canaan his eleven brothers were barely staying alive. Their former jealousy and strife toward Joseph now pierced them. Their security lay drought-stricken. And they with no goals for which to cling. This story illustrates the tragedy of settling for second best. The person who concedes his dreams is headed for trouble indeed. Endless wandering, unfulfillment, insecurity are his lot. Personal stagnation results.

In my Charlotte home we have a seventeen-car garage with everything from a brand-spanking-new Rolls Royce to an old classic, priceless silver streak model. Sometimes I'll think of the faces of my used-car customers and pat the hood, "Now here's one you'll really like," I'll say with a big smile. No sir, I didn't mind starting at the bottom at all. In a sense I'm still there because to fulfill my dreams I have a long way to go, spiritually as well as materially. Like Joseph, I am determined not to allow anyone to steal my dreams.

"Stop and think, everything we touch is the result of dreams come true!"

Dexter and Birdie Yager with President George Bush.

Dexter and Birdie Yager with Bob Hope.

14

Dexter and Birdie Yager with Ronnie Milsap.

Dexter and Birdie Yager with Art Linkletter.

16

Dexter Yager with Paul Harvey.

Dexter and Birdie Yager with William Shatner.

Dexter and Birdie Yager with Zig Ziglar — noted author and speaker.

Dexter and Birdie Yager with Debbie Reynolds.

2

◆◆◆

DON'T TRY IT, DO IT

Real success is not to be taken for granted. The achievement of our goals, if of any value to begin with, is no minor undertaking. If you do not have to work to accomplish a goal, then probably there was not much validity to it in the first place. Anything of value is worth exerting effort to obtain.

Half-hearted efforts bring less desirable outcomes. Once you decide upon a goal, step out and with every resource available, strive to reach it. Remember that the closer you get to success the harder it is to reach it. At first it might come easy. But somewhere along the way you will struggle.

An expectant mother finds it fairly easy in the first few months of her pregnancy to carry her child. The real test of endurance comes in the labor room at the hospital. Some women spend hours in labor. As time draws closer pressures build, the climax is hard to reach. Finally, with one thrustful effort new birth comes. Our strong determination and many times painful exertion, will give birth to our long sought after goals.

When Jean Francois Gravelet walked a tight rope across Niagara Falls in 1855 his attitude to begin with was not "I'll try it. I think I can do it." His attitude was "I can do it." The slightest bit of doubt might have cost him his life. The word "try" does not belong in the realm of successful living. It is an "in-between" word that implies doubt. It should rank among the list of swear words that children are punished for using. In essence, what it says is, "I probably can do it, but I better not because I might fail." Learning to play the piano takes time, diligence and determination. If you approach the bench with the attitude that you are going to *try* to learn, you automatically defeat your intentions. Say to yourself, "Even though it does not happen immediately, I will learn to master the piano."

God does not allow you to comprehend anything you cannot achieve. However, this does not mean that it will be achieved easily. We are only as big as our minds allow us to be. A little child might thrill over the idea of becoming a fireman or school teacher someday, but the real test comes when the requirements are weighed.

Our lives are built on what our environment has dictated to us. Some people cannot escape their environment. Their dreams are only an escape. They never consider that it can really happen. They have tunnel vision, and unless they expand their horizons, their children, too, will grow up the same way. What is extraordinary is that our dreams are built upon the knowledge we receive from our immediate surroundings and acquaintances. In light of this, there is no reason why we cannot see our dreams become reality. They are within reach. Don't be an idealist who never moves into action and don't be a defeatist who will only achieve the easiest goals.

Don't try it, do it. That leaves no room for failure. Allow

yourself no alternative dreams. Why be anything less than totally satisfied with yourself and your accomplishments? There is no reason why you have to live below your capabilities. A person who lives below what he is actually capable of performing is a most unhappy person. He is constantly plagued by his apparent failures. He always weighs the greatness of other's feats in light of his littleness. He draws himself into a shell, refusing to overcome the obstacles in his way.

This book was written to give the "try-ers" stronger incentive to "do" in their lives. Hopefully, all who read this will realize that unlimited possibilities lie ahead of them as they purpose to live out their dreams. One underlying fact always must remain: a dream unrealized is a dream imprisoned by that enemy of all enemies "the fear of failure." Set your dreams free by determining that you will see it happen.

At my Free Enterprise Day last year, my co-author, Doug Wead, made a surprising confession. "I used to always say, 'try' " he admitted to 40,000 salesmen. "Starting is one of the hardest steps to take! Just try. Get moving! But Dexter Yager has changed my vocabulary.

"There is a fascinating verse in the Bible. It contains the dying words of King David. It is interesting that we hear no sermons or sing no songs about these words. When you hear them you will think that they come from some modern version of the Bible. It's as if they had been placed in an incubator and passed down to this one generation to hear for the first time. The words are as relevant and as powerful as the most recent and dynamic Madison Avenue advertising scheme.

"King David was dying with only a dream of a great temple. The temple that would become the seventh wonder of the world. He had gathered the gold and the timber. He looked up into the eyes of his son Solomon and said before his deatʰ *'be strong, and be of good courage, and do it!'* "

Dexter and Birdie Yager with George Kennedy.

Dexter Yager with J.D. Sumner of J.D. Sumner and the Stamps

Dexter and Birdie Yager with Dr. and Mrs. Norman Vincent Peale.

Dexter and Birdie Yager with Pat Boone.

"Remember that the closer you get to success, the harder it is to reach."

"Be strong and be of good courage, and **do it!**"

1 Chronicles 28:20

3

ASSOCIATE WITH WINNERS

Your closest friends will brand you as a winner or loser. The crowd you associate with will determine what people think of you. Unlike the electrical charges in a battery, opposites do not attract. You feel most comfortable with people like you. Those who have similar interests, opinions, and life styles most easily win your friendship. Those who constantly build you up and share in your aspirations are the ones to which you like to cling. Joseph, ruler in the Egyptian domain, learned this the hard way. He thought his brothers were his best friends. Surely they would share his dreams. He experienced a rude awakening, however, upon being sold into slavery. Without realizing it, circumstances back-fired and Joseph's brothers caused him to become a winner by disassociating themselves with him.

Learn to associate with winners. If your best friend hinders you from reaching your goals, drop him. Sound hard? Maybe to some, but ironically, that step will probably help not only you, but help him as well. Joseph's brothers, after many years of strife, were actually helped by what had taken place.

We live in a very mobile society. We change jobs often, become involved in countless community, civic and religious organizations, change our place of residence frequently, and lose old friends to new acquaintances. Although many of these friendship changes can be attributed to physical and geographical reasons, there still remains the fact that as our goals change, so do our relationships. This might sound cruel, but accept it as a part of life's maturing process. That boy or girl you befriended in high school probably could not be your best friend today. That college roommate, although still holding a warm place in your heart, probably could not be your best friend today. Time, and the readjustments of our goals tend to change our feelings towards those with whom we associate. This sounds almost inhumane, but there will always be a change with those to whom you need to associate. Do not begrudge the fact, accept it as a challenge, allowing your associations to better you as a person. Your former associates and friends too, will meet new acquaintances and the process will begin anew for them as well.

How do friends and acquaintances help you reach your goals? First and foremost, everyone needs friendship. I'm not talking about a friend today and gone tomorrow. You need someone who will be your friend in good times and bad. Someone who will be your friend when the chips are down.

I used to work in a brewery in upstate New York. Like anyone else I felt the need for friendship. Most of my acquaintances at that time drank heavily. In that position it was easy to become an alcoholic. It got to the point where I was drinking up to two cases of beer a day. I soon realized that these men really were not my friends. They cared for me only as long as I was their drinking buddy. Off the job I realized my ill-led assumptions.

Because of our human element and dependence upon one another, our dreams, out of necessity, are built around each other. Martin Luther King realized that his dreams depended upon the cooperation of men and women everywhere. He said, "I have a dream that one day this nation will rise up and live out the true meaning of its creed: 'We hold these truths to be self-evident, that all men are created equal.'" The fulfillment of that dream depended upon wide scale cooperation of millions. (That might be an example of unrealistic dreaming. Prejudism and racial violence still remain top news stories today.)

For quick results dreams need to be built around a compact group of associations. To be a winner you need to associate with winners. To become successful you need to first acquaint yourself with success. Develop relationships with those who can help you obtain your goals, your dreams. That is not politics. Common sense and self-motivation principles legislate that advice. When I began in business for myself I felt it necessary and important to associate myself with those who could wisely advise me.

Develop relationships that will mutually edify both parties. Do not expect to take if you are not willing to give in return. The richest people are those who are always willing to give without honestly expecting anything in return. Not only is this concept Judeo-Christian, it is one of the laws that govern human affairs where men live peacefully, unitedly and succeed.

Your relationships, whether with your wife, your children, your colleagues, or neighbors, are intended for your benefit. In one respect they are a means to an end. If they are not helping you to become a better person then perhaps adjustments are in order. What's worse, if your associates are succeeding and you are not, then something is terribly wrong. There is nothing worse than seeing the other guy succeeding when you, a so-called friend, stand unfulfilled. Relationships are like two-way streets. Each party has his own goals and abilities, but must be

31

willing, in passing, to allow room for the other one to grow and succeed.

Our associations with people allow us to become better acquainted with ourselves and help direct us toward our dreams. If the time comes that this growth stops, then it is time to begin afresh. This is not "friend-hopping" or even a broken relationship. It simply points toward the fact that most non-domestic relationships eventually give out and are replaced by those which help to propagate our goals and dreams. Relationships *can* become stalemate.

Everyone has one or two people he names as a best friend. These people are key elements in the development and fulfillment of our dreams. They not only share in our aspirations and joys, but help us in tangible ways to reach those goals.

A young man was preparing to leave for college in another state. Days prior to leaving he was invited to his pastor's home. With excitement the minister and his wife discussed his aspirations and future plans. Looking him straight in the eyes the wife said, "Don't ever settle for second best. God knows your dreams and goals. He knows who your wife will be. He knows where you are headed." And again she emphasized, "Never settle for second best." Those words followed him throughout his college career. Major decisions in his life were made with those words always pervading his thoughts. That pastor's wife gave him incentive not to allow anyone to deter him from reaching his goals. She was a friend, instrumental in causing that boy to continue striving for his dreams.

If someone is not valuable to me as far as my goals are concerned, does this give me license to disassociate myself with them? Not hardly. It does however, provide me with a gauge as far as determining where my vital relationships are to be built.

Professional fund raisers do not spend their time on nickel and dime customers, but go where the money lies. They realize that their greatest assets lie in big money areas. The same is true for relationships. The successful person associates with those who will accentuate his life and support his dreams. This does not take away from the importance of any one man. It simply acknowledges the many levels of human aspiration and motivation.

If you are not satisfied with your cluster of friends, make the great "break away" and pursue relationships that will help you to usher into reality your long awaited dreams.

Sounds cruel, I know. I can hear your many objections on religious and moral grounds. I see no inconsistency. There is a difference between showing kindness to negative people and embracing their philosophy. According to sociologists, the number one factor leading to criminal and anti-social behavior is association. As parents we are very concerned with our children's friends. What about our friends? Do we leave their presence uplifted and encouraged? Remember, for all our moralizing, the Bible itself teaches that someday God will separate the winners from the losers. Spiritually, association means everything and in the physical, material world the same principle applies.

"A mirror reflects a man's face, but what he is really like is shown by the kind of friends he chooses."

—Proverbs 27:19 (Living Bible)

33

Dexter Yager with Roy Clark.

Dexter and Birdie Yager with Peter Vidmar — 1984 Olympic Gold Medalist.

Dexter and Birdie Yager with President Gerald Ford.

Dexter and Birdie Yager with Tammye Wynette.

Dexter and Birdie Yager with Lynda Carter.

Dexter Yager with Billy Dee Williams.

"Relationships are like two-way streets. Each party has his own goals and abilities, but must be willing, in passing, to allow room for the other one to grow and succeed."

To become successful, you need to first acquaint yourself with success."

4

GOALS: OUR STEPPING STONES

Well defined and properly pursued goals direct your life. No one can set your goals for you. Goal setting is a personal matter, and something that does not happen overnight. We set our goals and build on them day by day, week by week, month by month, year by year. A strong foundation, if layed carefully, eventually leads to the attainment of our goals. Like in a building project, the foundation must be strong and well constructed in order to allow for future planning and additions.

The fulfillment of a dream comes through high, yet realistic range setting. In order to succeed and reach our dreams, three goals have to be established. First, long range goals need to be decided upon. An individual needs to make up his mind as to what his long range goal is going to be, and then set a short range goal. Short range goals provide a means to the end.

When I first started out into business on my own I set a long range goal that I wanted to make one thousand dollars per month. This seems silly now, but big money then. My short range goal was to reinvest in my business for a period of one year and never look at the profits. I was going to be totally committed. It is very important that one be a "long ranger" when starting out.

An overweight person decides to go on a diet. He finds this especially crucial. He sets as his goal the loss of fifty pounds within a year's time. The loss of weight does not come overnight. Thousands of weight watchers will testify to that fact. That person then needs to set a realistic short range goal. Perhaps a realistic short range goal would be to lose four pounds a month.

The short range goals are extremely important. Unfortunately, many people ignore this category. Even those who take the time often set their short range goals too high, so high that they become unreachable. There are two areas by which the short range setter can gauge himself. First of all you have to know yourself, know what your strengths and limitations are. Men have realized the importance of this for centuries. The Greek philosopher Socrates said, "To thyself be true." In other words, know what you can do and what you cannot do. Do not try to accomplish a feat that you possibly cannot do. Be realistic with yourself and with others.

Our society says that going to college will raise a person's income. Do not go to college because of what society says, go to college because it fits into your specific plans. We were not meant to be societal robots. Neither can we afford to be dishonest with ourselves. It is very important that you pinpoint your own interests and capabilities and go from there. Realistic short range planning ultimately ushers into reality our long range goals.

Secondly, you have to stop and ask yourself, "What am I

willing to pay to reach my goal?" Many times long hours and leisurely sacrifices will be required to accomplish one's goals. Jesus said that before beginning one must, "count the cost."

In light of my long range and short range goals, what am I doing to build for tomorrow? That is the question you must ask yourself. The establishing of immediate goals is just as important as long range and short range planning. The fulfillment of dreams is a gradual process and needs to be worked out on a day by day basis. The establishment of immediate goals provides the stairway that reaches to the fulfillment of long range planning.

What happens when you reach the goal that you have striven for? Is that where it ends?

Not hardly. For when one has reached a long sought goal that is only the beginning of a new adventure. When a goal is fulfilled that automatically gives you license to set a new goal for yourself. Pursue it even stronger.

Do not go into neutral. Like in driving a standard car, you've got to decide when to shift again. The same thing pertains to our goals. Once you've reached a goal decide then to shift toward something bigger and better.

"The establishment of immediate goals provides the stairway that reaches to the fulfillment of long range planning."

Dexter and Birdie Yager with Mike Wallace — CBS 60 Minutes.

Dexter Yager with Brenda Lee.

*"A strong foundation,
if layed carefully,
eventually leads
to the attainment
of our goals."*

Dexter and Birdie Yager with Dr. David Swartz
(author of The Magic of Thinking Big.)

5

BE A WINNER, NOT A WHINER

People find it easy many times to blame others for their shortcomings and failures. Although deep inside they realize that they only are to blame, self-pity and pride dominate their ability to admit it. It is far easier to place the blame elsewhere and hide behind a false front. A person of this low status can be best defined as a whiner. A whiner is never wrong. Whenever misfortune comes his way he skillfully finds a convenient loophole and traces the blame back to someone else in that same situation. A whiner always takes the easy way out. Those about him see right through him, and though they might associate with him, possess no respect for him.

Children many times enter into whiny periods of life. When their requests are not met by their parents, when their friends surpass them in certain areas, they many times become whiners. They constantly complain or tearfully beg for sympathy in an indignant manner.

A whining child is an obnoxious child. He needs to be taught that not everything comes easy. He will not necessarily get that new baseball glove or that new barbie doll. Although a whiny child is obnoxious, his age at least allows us to partially understand why he acts the way he does.

What is more obnoxious however, is to see a full grown whiner. Young whiners, if not set straight early enough, grow into big whiners.

The manager of a sales company was training a new group of employees. He discussed the company's sales program and policies in an easy-to-understand manner. Upon completion of his talk, he made the comment, "I don't mind bottle-feeding you guys to begin with, but when it gets to the place where I have to part your whiskers to stick the bottle in your mouth, that's carrying it a bit too far." What was he saying? Learn to stand on your own two feet. If you fall in the first attempt get up and try again. Don't blame it on someone else. Confront yourself with the failures and determine to go at it harder the next time.

Sad to say, some people seem doomed to lose in whatever they do. A dark gray thundercloud follows them wherever they go. They become imitations of the popular cartoon character, "The born loser." They are always the butt of someone's joke, and end up losing their self-worth and dignity. A whiner falls into the category of those people with whom you need to disassociate yourself. You place not only yourself, but your dreams in jeopardy by associating with whiners. Obviously, they have no constructive goals for which to cling. They cannot command themselves, how can they ever hope to reach their goals?

Whining should be placed in the terminal disease category. It is a disease that takes away from a person's self-worth and destroys his chances of success. Whiners do not succeed, they simply exist.

This dreaded disease can be recognized through the observance of several symptoms. A whiner, ironically, is always right, or so he thinks. Regardless of what the majority might say he refuses to give in. In so doing he makes a complete fool of himself.

Two baseball teams with a tied score were nearing the end of the sixth inning. The team at bat had two outs and the bases were loaded. Tension was high as the batter smacked the ball into center field, too high for the shortstop's reach. With lightning speed the ball was scooped up and hurled toward homeplate. The catcher snatched the ball and in the nic of time tagged the third base runner out. No immediate questions were asked about the umpire's decision, as the teams prepared to enter into another inning of play. All of a sudden, a loud voice was heard above the noise of the crowd. A rookie player was yelling, "he's not out, what do you mean he's out, ump?" Silence pervaded. The young man continued to challenge the call until finally, his coach told him to sit down and cool off. For the remainder of the game he was heard whining loudly in the dugout, and constantly harassing the umpire's every call. He was right and no one else was going to tell him any different.

This characteristic of a whiner goes hand and hand with the fact that the other person is always at fault. Never is the blame to be placed upon himself. His character will not allow him to admit his personal shortcomings.

Another symptom of a whiner includes his lack of motivation. His actions go as far as the sound waves that carry them. The only art he has successfully mastered is complaining, griping, and losing. As a result of his poor self-image and his shortcomings, the whiner becomes extremely obnoxious. His real friends are few in number. Tendencies develop to overcompensate for shortcomings, thus making the whiner unbearable to live with. The whiner is like a car spinning on an icy road, making a lot of noise but getting nowhere fast.

In a nutshell, there are three classes of people: losers, leaners and leaders. Losers never succeed. They are defeated even before they begin. Losers insist that they cannot reach their dreams. To them dreams are intangible ideals that are not meant to be fulfilled. They live in a fantasy world. They fantasize grandeurs of success, chart their course toward fame and wealth, but when reality strikes them, they lose all hope, stagnate, and once again become whiners. Losers are usually beyond hope. They make their minds up quickly. Rather than enticing them, real success haunts them.

Leaners are wishy washy. If things are going smooth they are alright. About the time problems develop in reaching their goals, they stay back and concede their dreams to someone else. If confronted with challenge they always are willing to settle for second best. These kind of people straddle the fence. When the grass is thick and green they are like a fat cow enjoying its food. But when the bull charges they jump over the fence and settle for last season's crop without giving it a fight.

There is absolutely no room for losers or leaners in the realm of successful living. Successful people are leaders. They possess leadership capabilities. They have full confidence in their abilities to lead into those areas destined for their success. Leaners annoy them, so they endeavor to make leaders out of them. They recognize their own shortcomings and weaknesses and build around them.

Finally, leaders are winners. A winner is one who accepts his failures and mistakes, picks up the pieces, and continues striving to reach his goals. The winner is not afraid to tackle what is seemingly impossible. He accepts it for what it is—a challenge. And he does not stop until that challenge has been met. Unlike the whiner, he shouts cheers of accomplishment. He always runs on the winning streak, jumping obstacles, and exerting whatever it takes to reach his dreams.

The whiner remains in the starting blocks dredding the sound of the gun. The leaner wants to win, but is not quite willing to put forth the required effort. But the winner will after a hard struggle, rip through the finish line, receiving as his award the fulfillment of his dreams.

"The leaner wants to win, but is not quite willing to put forth the required effort."

53

Dexter and Birdie Yager with Phyllis Diller.

Dexter and Birdie Yager with Louise Mandrell.

*"A winner
is one who accepts
his failures and mistakes,
picks up the pieces,
and continues striving
to reach his goals."*

To Dexter Yager
With best wishes,
Ronald Reagan

Dexter Yager with President Ronald Reagan.

Dexter Yager with Denis and Susan Waitley
(author of Seeds of Greatness.)

6

DEVELOP A GOOD SELF-IMAGE

"What you see is what you get!" This popular phrase touches upon a thought provoking truth as far as individuals are concerned. Hopefully, this phrase is used by those who know who they are, and know where they are headed. It is coined by those who realize they have flaws, yet are striving to correct those flaws. In no way is it egotistical. If you cannot or do not think well of yourself, how do you expect some one else to? If you believe that you cannot do something, then how do you expect others to believe you can? During a job interview you would not inform the employer that you probably cannot do what is required of you, but are willing to give it a try. That is absurd, and in that case, would put you back in the unemployment line.

Listen to this ancient, familiar, but powerful proverb, "As a man thinketh in his heart so is he." What you think, is what you are. Thinking and being go hand in hand. Remember that successful people are always willing to do what the failure is too good to do.

Look at your life. Evaluate yourself in light of what you are today and what you could be tomorrow. Sort out the good from the bad. With that finished, determine to better the bad and to completely utilize the good in your life. When someone does not like me, I consider that to be their problem. Some people will not like you regardless of what you do or who you are. A sad fact of life is that not everyone is going to like you. If you can honestly admit that you have faults and are working to improve them, then you do not need to worry about what people think or say about you. Then if they do not like you that is their problem.

Take adequate time to do your self-evaluation, to look at those areas in your life that need to be improved. If something bothers you do something about it. If you are overweight and it bothers you, get on a diet and lose it. If you are going bald and it embarrasses you, get a toupee. And remember, if you are satisfied with the way you look, do not let people bother you about it. If something does not bother you, then certainly you should not let people bother you about it. You have to live with you. And no one else.

What we think of ourselves will show in several areas of our life. Our conversations can be either seasoned with self-assurance and pleasantry or negativity and monotony. A person who has full control of himself and has full confidence in what he can do, will demonstrate these traits in his conversation. Have you ever talked with someone who kept apologizing for who he is or what he said? An apologetic person is a pathetic person, entangled within his own snare of belittlement.

One young man went into a small clothing store to sell advertisements for a community newspaper. Having very little confidence in himself, and not really believing in the product he was promoting, the young man ended up apologizing to the manager for taking up his valuable time. The manager was instantly turned off because of the salesman's poor self-image and apologetic attitude. The young man lost not only the sale but lowered his self-esteem.

Most of us when acknowledged for our noteable accomplishments, become embarrassed, frustrated and even mad. We lower our self-image by putting ourselves down and saying, "No, I didn't do that, it really didn't take much work." We cower like a sheep before a lion. If a person is used to being put down by his friends, parents or whomever, even after he has accomplished a feat, then he should run from that negative feedback. If a child grows up never being commended for what he does he develops a tendency when full grown to be very negative, and accordingly, a very negative self-image. If those with whom you associate are constantly in the habit of putting you down, get away from them. Choose friends who will build you up, and who will become accessories to reaching your dreams. Choose associates who will help to program your computer in a positive manner.

The way a person dresses provides an excellent clue as to what he thinks of himself. Loose, wrinkled clothes suggest to the onlooker a lack of ambition and constructive goal setting. That person probably thinks very low of himself. Perhaps a great deal of this is subconscious but modern surveys of America's greatest businessmen show that the way you dress tells a lot about you.

The last two decades have brought with them countless and rapid changes in clothing styles. In the late sixties mini skirts were on the scene. Most young women in the country wore them. Pant suits for women gained popularity in the early 1970's. And again the majority wore them. In the late 70's three-pieced suits are big among men. Women are now wearing dresses common to those seen in the early 30's. The cycle continues.

Again our society has programmed people to change with

61

the fads. Many people appear in public making complete fools of themselves because their clothing does not fit their body shape or their personality. Obese women in mini skirts, very skinny men in three-pieced suits, unusually tall women wear four inch heels, older men wear high-heeled shoes. The way you dress is a very personal matter, but keep in mind that the same style was not made for everyone. When you make a business call make sure you look like a businessman. If a three-pieced suit does not look well on you wear a suit that does. Appropriately, you will feel more successful if dressed properly.

Attitude is another asset or hindrance to a good self-image. An "I-can't-do-it" attitude immediately brands you as having a negative self-image. If you think you cannot do something, then chances are you won't be able to. Attitude stems from your frame of mind. Psychologists and theologians readily agree that the sub-conscious mind or "the heart" completely controls our actions and deeds. Attitude is a factor in our personality. From this comes our likes and dislikes toward people and things. A person's attitude will either make him friends or make him an outcast. Naturally, people do not like to be around someone who has a negative attitude. In part, a good self-image comes from having a healthy attitude about yourself and about your capabilities. Success is imminent for the person who says, "I can do it," and then has no after-thoughts of doubt.

A person with a good self-image works hard. He takes his work seriously and does a good job. He goes the extra mile to insure complete satisfaction. He realizes that the quality of his work is a direct reflection on him as a person. A top-notch businessman will work extra hours to insure satisfied customers. A track star will run an extra mile during practice to secure tomorrow's victory. Hard work is the requirement for the person striving to be successful. Tough times will come, but keeping your goal in view, dig your heels in deeper and work harder to meet the challenge.

62

The importance of a good self-image cannot be stressed enough. Only a few of the areas that influence your self-image have been discussed. No matter what your occupation, your status in the community, or your personal ambitions a good self-image will keep you going when circumstances say, "Stop!"

"A good self-image will keep you going when circumstances say STOP!"

Dexter and Birdie Yager with Tom Smothers.

"A person with **Confidence** will demonstrate that in his conversation."

Dexter Yager with Donna Mills.

"Remember that successful people are willing to do what the failure is too good to do!"

Dexter and Birdie Yager with Henry Mancini.

7

MONEY MANAGEMENT

"Money isn't everything, but it sure helps!" This often quoted remark does possess some validity. Let's face it, in our economy money is important. A well rounded income is essential to comfortable living. And naturally, there are evils in money.

The Bible says that the root of all evil is the love of money, not money, but the love of money. If money becomes an obsession in our lives then we need to reassess our priorities. If money stands in the way of our personal happiness or that of our families, then re-evaluation of our priorities are definitely in order. However, we have got to get it out of our minds that money is evil. Money is not evil, it is a necessity. Just like the air we breathe, it is not evil, it is necessary in order to function adequately.

This is not to imply that successful people are necessarily rich people. Very definitely, you can be successful without possessing extreme wealth. It may be that your goals do not require financial backing. Certainly, not everything in this world necessitates money to acquire. The most important things of life cannot be purchased with money. Necessities such as love, happiness, security cannot be bought. You cannot find these on any store counter or in any mail order catalogue.

Money then, does not make people rich. A wealthy person is rich only if he is willing to better himself, but more than that, to better the lives that touch him. The attainment of our goals always involves more than ourselves. It involves probably a countless number of people. Money is definitely not the key factor.

The popular television series, "The Waltons" amply illustrates the fact that money does not make people rich. Producer, writer Earl Hammer vividly portrays a financially struggling family during the depression years. In the Walton home money is scarce. Hand-me-downs, barefoot schoolers, and other materialistic sacrifices are common. Although they are not rich financially speaking, they are rich in family love. A strong family unity bound together by love, carries the family through the hard depression years. Indeed, in that respect, they were rich.

Looking at it from the other end of the spectrum, there is absolutely nothing wrong with bringing home a large paycheck or business profits. More important than making money is *how* we make our money, and what we do with it after we get it. No, money does not buy intangible items. Money will buy you a new car, a new home, a new yacht and even a new heart, but it will not buy the psychological and inherent human necessities of life.

World reknown Howard Hughes was a millionaire many times over. He had everything and anything that men dream about possessing. There was no material possession that he could not obtain had he wanted to. However, Howard Hughes was one of the loneliest men that ever lived. He died a recluse, and in the most important respect, filthy poor.

Scripture says that a steward should be found faithful. What does this mean? Be wise as to how you spend your money. Do not waste your money. Spend it for worthy items. Teenagers many times are guilty of "blowing" their money. Last year millions of dollars were spent by teenagers for items listed in the "junk" category. Teenagers are notoriously described as spendthrifts. Money is not intended to be spent unwisely, but some businesses flourish for that reason alone. Money management needs to be instilled within people if they are to reach those goals that require financial backing. Children, especially, are spendthrifts. When given a quarter a child immediately must spend it. That attitude in later life could hinder the fulfillment of a dream.

When asked about the purpose for money one automatically replies, "To spend." It is simple, or is it? As a rule, that is true, but what about the relationship money plays in the attainment of our goals? Surely you will agree that money is instrumental in helping us to reach our goals. It is very probable that your dreams are tangible, goals you can both see and touch. If managed correctly our money will provide opportunities that otherwise could not unfold. Good money management is essential to the fulfillment of our dreams. Good money management propagated the success that Yager Enterprises is now experiencing.

If your dream is to go into business for yourself, then certainly money will be needed. If your dream is to build a new two-story home, then without question, money is needed. A dream of making $50,000 a year goes without question! This sounds redundant, but it is something a lot of people do not think about. Instant and free success comes only in fairy tales and love stories. Successful people need to learn how to manage their money. A spendthrift has nothing upon which to build. There again, money is not everything but it sure helps!

Good money management should be enjoyable. Ideally, we should enjoy making our money as much as we enjoy spending it. If this is not the case our work becomes sheer drudgery. A person who does not enjoy making his money is a discontented person. All across our nation millions of men work in factories and small shops. Day after day they go to work, many of them dreading the sound of the alarm. Work time once again has arrived and they go out the door painstakingly dreading the day's events. On their way to work they already long for the quitting bell to sound. Each day is a new eternity to them. Time is punishment and seems futile. How sad. These men literally waste away their lives doing something they are not at all happy with. Sure enough, many of them have no alternative, but there are some who if they really wanted to, could change their predicament.

If you do not enjoy making your money then perhaps you need to change jobs. Perhaps you are in the wrong business. Life is too short to waste time on doing things we really do not enjoy. Sure, there will be things in this life that are musts, and that we will not necessarily like to do, but these do not have to translate into day after day affairs.

We enjoy our business. Yager Enterprises is our life. And we enjoy money management. We are now able to take vacations more frequently and enjoy them, but vacations are not what we really enjoy. They are nice, but our business spells joy and fulfillment to us. Our dreams lie in what we do each day, and each day we work to surpass what we already have.

74

"Remember this is your vision— It is the product of your own subconscious. It is almost an instinct. Trust it!"

*"A wealthy
person is rich
only if he is willing
to better himself,
but more than that,
to better the lives
that touch him."*

President Jimmy Carter.

*"Money
will buy you a new car,
a new home,
a new yacht
and even a new heart,
but it will not buy
the psychological and
inherent human
necessities of life."*

To Dexter & Birdie Yager
With deepest appreciation Ronald Reagan
for your generosity & support

President Ronald Reagan.

President Richard Nixon.

80

8

DON'T GET HUNG
BY YOUR TONGUE

The tongue, although one of the smallest members of our body, has the ability to determine the fulfillment or unfulfillment of our dreams. Either way, what we say has a great impact upon what we actually do. The person who says, "I can't do it" is defeated even before he begins. He "hangs" himself by his tongue!

One saying goes, "what you confess, you possess." If a person frequently repeats that he is sick, chances are he will actually become sick. Mind in cooperation with the tongue can actually bring something to pass. Doctors have reported cases where individuals imagined and confessed that they were sick, and always complained about their supposed infirmity. After thorough examinations nothing found to substantiate the described sickness. Still, the person said he was sick. What he confessed he possessed.

In one sense, the tongue has slain more people than all the armies that have marched upon the earth. Countless multitudes have been victim to its slashing remarks. Psychologically, lives have been destroyed by the tongue. In just a matter of seconds a person's life can be crushed by this all-powerful instrument. Scripture tells us that the tongue has the ability, if not controlled, to issue out poison. If a tongue is not bridled, that poison will enter into the mainstream of a life and deaden it. How many dreams have been destroyed because of someone's unruly tongue? Countless thousands! The tongue has implanted doubt, fear, discouragement into the lives of many dreamers. Many times those around us—our friends, neighbors, families, destroy our dreams. Without realizing it they lessen our chances of success. A person who cannot control his tongue is a person who has no constructive goals. His life is one of misery and he preys on the dreams and goals of others. Unfortunately, many allow the harsh words of these miserable people to rob them of their God-given dreams. You can also be victim to your own tongue. Never forget that. What you say has a lot of bearing upon what you do. You can hang yourself. You can poison yourself. That is why it is important to remember one piece of advice: Put your mind in gear before you talk. Think about what you are going to say and how it will affect those to whom you are addressing yourself. If a car is parked on a hillside and left in neutral it will roll and crash. Tragic consequences may result. The same goes for neutral tongues. Our remarks, if not geared in a positive direction, may cause damage. What takes seconds to say might take years to heal. Broken homes, family feuds, friendships have all been destroyed because someone did not think before they spoke.

Remember that your tongue is second in command. First of all, the mind legislates what we say and do. Then the mind puts our tongue into gear. So the real damage is done in the mind first, and then the orders are carried out by the use of our tongue. Nevertheless, we can still get hung by our tongue.

A person who cannot control his tongue is a person who probably will not succeed in life. His tongue not only destroys his personal chances for success, but also slashes the dreams of others.

Confessing that you cannot do something is the mark of a loser. Confession brings possession, and in that case, brings bitter disappointment.

*"The person who says,
'I can't do it'
is defeated
even before he begins."*

President George Bush.

9

THE WOMEN BEHIND THE MAN

In the Biblical account, God created the beauties around us; the earth, the heavens, the fowl and animals, the plant life and sea and declared that it was good. Then He created man and said it was not good—he needed a help-mate. So woman came into being, to complete the man.

It has been said that behind every good man is a good woman, and a remarkable Harvard University survey proves that that corny old adage may be more profound then we realize. "A woman can make or break a man" is another comment often heard. It is true that she can make him feel like a giant or the proverbial 'mouse.' Many times women tend to forget the power they hold in the man-woman relationship. A word of encouragement or a tender touch can make a man feel ten feet tall and ready to conquer the world and yet, just as easily, a nagging word and cool attitude can make him a total failure. A woman can play a key role in retarding or stimulating a man's career. If she goes into marriage with her mind set on competing for the position of power, conflict after conflict will result.

Some corporations are now sponsoring marriage seminars because they realize a person is more productive if he or she is winning at home. A business analyst for Associated Press says: "Companies cannot develop male managers without the wife's support."

I have good news for those men and women who love each other. The J. Paul Getty and Henry Ford myth suggests that great financial success comes at the expense of the wife and children. The myth has been that a successful career results in a marriage failure, and health and spiritual problems as well. But what we have recently learned shows that this is not true.

Town and Country magazine recently commissioned a Harvard study of the 100 leading industrialists in the United States. A surprising discovery was that 90 were married to their first wife, and eight of the remaining ten were married to their second wife and had been so for more then ten years. This is striking news and let me remind you how high above average divorce statistics these 100 men were.

This Harvard study suggests two things. One, success does not come in one area of life at the expense of the other. Success is contagious and once begun it spills over into every other area of life. Secondly, it takes two to make success. The leading industrialists of this country seem to have an extraordinary common denomination. They all have good wives.

But what can a wife do to strengthen her husband's career? Unless she met her husband through common work, she has probably drifted away from him in terms of his career and her own. Perhaps she has no career herself and is totally emersed in family and home activities. What can she do?

A very powerful force available is her own sexuality. A

woman can use sex negatively by playing psychological games with her husband. She can become a legal prostitute by using sex as a reward system. By withholding sex and love she can get her way. If he doesn't react in a situation as she thinks he should, she can get mad and sulk and withdraw her sexuality. With this mental-physical tug-of-war, many men leave the home and go out to combat the business world.

An alert and talented wife will recognize that through her own sexuality she has the power to impart a confidence and ego to her man that no other source can provide. Since he is working for her dreams as well as his own she is smart to help him along. I know, this sounds chauvenistic. This is not for everyone and it may anger many. The man has great responsibility within marriage and we usually are too insensitive to the woman's needs, but since I am not a woman I will not try to tell you about that. I am only explaining what happens to me and how I feel. The truth is, Birdie made me feel successful when I was nothing. She is my secret weapon.

Marriage is more than a 50-50 proposition. It is a 100% from each partner; working and striving for a harmonious relationship in the home, thus flowing out into the work day world. If a woman really works at understanding her husband's needs, he, in turn, will respond to her needs.

Sex is fulfilling and comforting—that special time when a man and woman come together as one. Tensions are relieved, pressures and cares are forgotten and love deepened. With that love comes faith, trust and belief in each other.

Marriage is not a down-hill experience; it should get better and better! It is a growing experience in love, security and freedom. Some have said that freedom to a man is *to do* what he has to do; what ever God has led Him to do. Freedom to a woman is *not to do*—such as not having to do everyday responsibilities and having someone to clean the house so that she has a day off. Success can be totally different to a man and a woman.

89

In our early years of marriage Birdie came to the realization of what freedom meant to me in my life. She said she felt that I ought to go fishing or swimming, go on picnics or to the movies and do all the nice things that show a person is successful and that we had the money to do it with. This was her idea of freedom for me. My idea of freedom was to "just get out there and do my thing"—to be able to try what I wanted to try and having her to stand with me.

A woman must think positive; believe in her husband and be willing to take a risk with him. She must allow him the latitude of making mistakes and misjudgments. In the marriage vows we repeat "for better, for worse; for richer, for poorer" and in our new wedded bliss we are unable to fully understand what life is really about. We plunge in and the icy waters of matrimony hit us and suddenly we realize the 'bed of roses' is no longer there. A woman can draw back in her own negative little world, dwarf her husband and smother their relationship; or she can think positive, believe in and support her husband and be willing to take a risk toward a new adventure in business.

Status is important to a woman. Many times it does something for the female ego to be the *doctor's* wife or the *dentist's* wife instead of just being the *wife*. In such a situation, you will usually find a miserable man, trying to make a good, successful image in the community just for the woman. When a woman gets her head on straight she will realize that her true status comes by fulfilling her role in her husband's life as the helpmate and companion, lover and partner. She must admire her husband for who he is and not only for what he does. Knowing this, the man will want to accomplish, to try new things, and strive for new goals.

Many times women are filled with fear for the unknown. Sometimes it gets to the point that she cannot let the man step out and do anything without her approval, or thinking it won't work. She can stifle him by mistrust—wanting to know what he's been doing, where he has been and who he has been seeing. This attitude can easily lead toward a "mother-son" role instead of a "husband-wife" role.

The woman behind the man IS a very important ingredient in his success. She can add spice or she can sour a relationship. If a couple is going to build a business together they must communicate in every area of life. Some couples may communicate in one or two areas of their lives and not the rest. Thus it takes them twice as long to get where they are going.

Remember the little train huffing and puffing up the steep mountain grade saying, "I thought I could—I thought I could—I thought I could!" A woman can give her husband the kind of encouragement and inspiration to believe he can do anything—going right to the top and having a great sense of satisfaction in knowing they did it together—to the top and beyond!

OTHER BOOKS
BY
DEXTER AND BIRDIE YAGER

Don't Let Anybody Steal Your Dream
Dexter Yager with Douglas Wead

This classic in the field of motivational writing has sold more than a million copies and is selling as well today as it did in 1978 when it was first published. Dexter Yager has influenced millions with his forthright honesty, compassion and desire to see others succeed. Here is a man who has "made it" in all the right ways, and who is willing to pour out the ideas that make for successful living.
Paperback: Stock No. BK-10
Spanish: Stock No. IBK-1

Becoming Rich
Dexter Yager and Doug Wead

Inspirational and moving stories of some of the world's greatest people and the eleven principles behind their success. Includes Walt Disney, Albert Einstein, Martin Luther King, Andrew Carnegie, Adolph Ochs, Jackie Robinson, Thomas Edison, Helen Keller, Harry Truman, Coco Chanel, Winston Churchill, Arturo Toscanini, and Douglas MacArthur.
Paperback: Stock No. BK-97

The Secret of Living is Giving
Birdie Yager with Gloria Wead

Birdie Yager, wife of one of America's most famous and powerful businessmen, talks about:
• Marriage: How to make it work.
• Attitude: The way to popularity and self-esteem.
• Your Husband: How to make him rich!
• Children: When to say no, and when to say yes.
• Health and Beauty: They are the result of decisions, and are not automatic.
• Money: When it is bad; when it can be wonderful.
• Faith in God: Why you must deal with your guilt and inferiority, or self-destruct.
Paperback: Stock No. BK-96

Millionaire Mentality
Dexter Yager with Doug Wead

At last! A book on financial responsibility by one of America's financial wizards, Dexter Yager! Dexter gives freely of his remarkable business acumen, teaching you how to take inventory and plan for financial independence.
Here is a common sense, down-to-earth book about investments, shopping, credit and car buying, and budgeting time and money.
Included are anecdotes about other successful American business people—to give you ideas about where to go from here!
If you are serious about financial planning, this is the book for you!
Paperback: Stock No. BK-206

The Business Handbook
Dexter Yager

The most comprehensive how-to-do-it manual ever offered!
A simple yet detailed guide that lets you chart your own path to success in Amway.
The Business Handbook brings you the best in proven techniques regardless of whether you want to earn just a little extra income or if you are interested in building a large successful organization.
Discover what MLM or Network Marketing (as revealed in Megatrends) really is and how it differs from Direct Marketing and Pyramiding.
Awaken yourself to the proven advantages offered through the Amway phenomenon.
Learn the importance of:
• Winning
• Leadership
• Goalsetting
• Loyalty
• Dreambuilding
Discover the secret techniques used by many successful distributors who have become millionaires and are fulfilling their greatest dreams.
Paperback: Stock No. BK-247

Successful Family Ties:
Developing Right Relationships for Lasting Success.
Ron Ball with Dexter Yager

Right Relationships with the people around you are fundamental to your success in life — emotionally, spiritually, and even in your work. This book will give you high performance, practical guidelines for dealing with the many important issues that may be holding you back from experiencing success in your family relationships. You'll learn to recognize the signs of trouble and to take steps toward overcoming.
• ruptured relationships
• busy signals in communication
• sexual temptation
• stress
• selfishness
• negative people
And with principles founded on God-given, timeless truths you'll discover lasting success in all your challenges and be sure to have successful family ties.
Hardback: Stock No. BK-310

A Millionaire's Common Sense Approach to Wealth
Dexter Yager with Ron Ball

Finally! A book that brings the sometimes complicated and misunderstood concept of wealth to the level of understanding of the common man. In a common sense, straight forward way, this millionaire shares his sometimes bold and very candid approach to accumulating wealth.
With all his experience in business and life in general he is indisputably a wise man. And with this wisdom and honesty he talks about:
> misconcepts about money and materialism, eleven reasons to be rich, the principles of: work, dreams, people, perseverance, and investment. He continues with information on breaking budget barriers, doing a personal financial analysis, developing a common sense about managing money, and the spiritual secret of true success.

Paperback: Stock No. BK-315

The Mark of A Millionaire
Dexter Yager and Ron Ball

Dexter Yager's financial accomplishments are world-renowned. Now his life principles are revealed in plain terms.

There is no mystery to success. It is achieved by those who understand its reasons. Here is a book filled with proven methods that will make your success happen!

- How do you specify a life target?
- What is a success plan?
- How do you overcome killer stress as you climb higher?
- Why is your personal image so vital?
- What is the key spiritual dimension in material accomplishment?
- How do you keep your success once you've won it?

The answers are in the pages of this book.

The Mark of a Millionaire is like attending a private graduate course in real-life achievement given by a man who has not only done it but continues to do it everyday.

These principles work!

Paperback: Stock No. BK-334

Everything I Know at the Top I Learned at the Bottom
Dexter Yager and Ron Ball

Personal stories and lessons from the life of Dexter Yager provide insights into the keys to success. Read about Dexter Yager's early boyhood experiences selling soda pop to construction workers; learn the important business principle he picked up from his early days selling cars. Out of these personal accounts from the life of a successful leader, you can learn valuable lessons for use in your career and your life.

Paperback: Stock No. BK-351

Available from your distributor, local bookstore, or write to:

Internet Services Corporation
P.O. Box 412080
Charlotte, NC 28241

Please include $5.00 for shipping and handling.